Incredible Insects

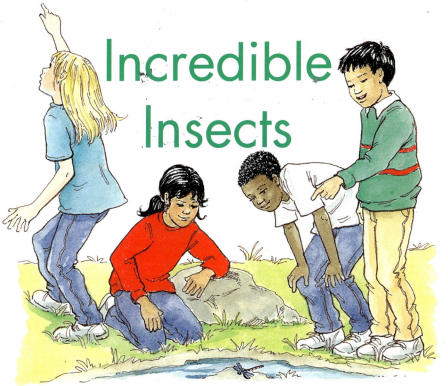

Helena Ramsay

Illustrated by
Jenny Mumford

Insects existed long before dinosaurs. More than 350 million years ago there were already insects living on the Earth.

4

Today there are approximately 30 million known **species** of insect in the world. Every year scientists discover new species that have never been seen before.

In this book we are going to look at incredible insects from all over the world.

Insects come in many thousands of different shapes and sizes. Some insects are so small that we have to look through a magnifying glass or microscope to see them properly. The smallest insect in the world is a kind of **parasite**. It is a wasp called the fairy fly, which is only 0.2 millimetres long.

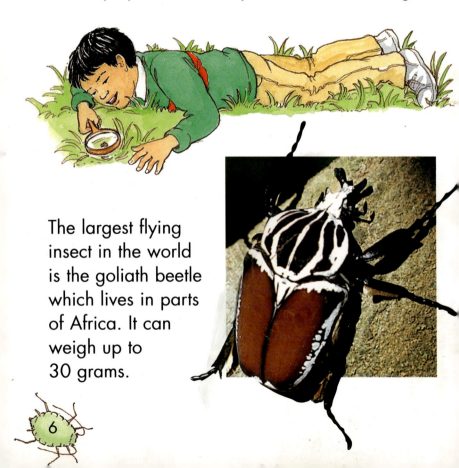

The largest flying insect in the world is the goliath beetle which lives in parts of Africa. It can weigh up to 30 grams.

Most large insects live in tropical climates.
The tropical walking stick lives in the trees and
shrubs of Brazil.

It looks just like a twig.

The tropical walking
stick can be over
30 centimetres long.

There are many different shapes and sizes of insect, but they all have three parts to their bodies and three pairs of legs.

Head

Thorax

Abdomen

8

This beautiful cicada from Malaysia has raised its wings over its back, which means we can hardly see its **abdomen**.

Why is it making that noise?

The male cicada 'sings' to attract a mate. He makes the sound with two 'drums' on his abdomen. These are made out of skin which the insect clicks in and out. The noise can be heard up to a kilometre away.

Unlike the cicada, many male moths are unable to call their mates; instead they are equipped with magnificent feathery **antennae**. This luna moth can use his antennae to pick up the scent of a female from a distance of several kilometres.

All insects have antennae on their heads. They use them for tasting and feeling as well as smelling.

Ants often feel each other's antennae when they meet. They can recognize ants from their own nest by touching them in this way. Insects with poor eyesight, like ants, often have particularly large antennae.

11

12

> *Look, that ant is stroking another insect.*

The ant is using its antennae to stroke a greenfly. When its abdomen is stroked the greenfly produces sweet honey-dew which the ant can drink. Some kinds of ant are rather like dairy farmers, they keep herds of greenfly for milking. In return for the honey-dew, the ants protect the greenflies' eggs from **predators** like ladybirds.

13

Dragonflies have very good eyesight, so their antennae are much smaller than those of the ant. Insects do not have simple eyes with a single **lens** like you and me. The dragonfly's enormous compound eyes are each made up of 30,000 lenses. Each lens receives a slightly different picture.

Isn't that a bit confusing?

All the pictures join together to create a single image in the insect's brain.

The dragonfly is a fierce and efficient hunter.
When flying it has a cruising speed of up to 50
kilometres per hour. It uses its enormous eyes to
see the other flying insects that are its **prey**. The
dragonfly's eyes are so large they meet in the
centre of its head.

15

All insects have enemies: some are eaten by other species of insect and others are prey to frogs, toads, lizards, snakes, birds and even mammals. In order to survive, insects must be able to defend themselves. Some are protected from predators by a nasty taste or smell and some are poisonous.

Poisonous insects usually have red or yellow and black markings. In the animal kingdom predators know that these are danger colours.

This moth is red and black, so it must be dangerous.

The colours of this cinnabar moth indicate that it is deadly poisonous. This means it can fly about by day without fear of being eaten.

Many insects use their colour, pattern or shape as a means of **camouflage**.

That's a very prickly twig!

These creatures look like part of
the twig but they are really thorn bugs.

This kind of camouflage is called mimicry, because the insects are imitating or mimicking the plants they live on.

Some non-poisonous insects mimic other species of insect that taste bad or have poisonous stings. Although this hoverfly looks like a wasp, it has no sting.

Some insects disguise themselves so that they can capture and eat other insects more easily. Can you see an insect in this picture?

I can see some mud and old leaves...

This is an assassin bug. It camouflages itself by sticking earth and leaves on its back. Disguised in this way, it can catch insects unawares and suck them dry of their body fluids.

The tiger beetle lives in desert regions. It is probably the fiercest of all the **carnivorous** feeders. The adult beetle is the fastest-moving insect in the world. It can chase its victims at a speed of 60 centimetres per second.

21

Not only are insects masters of disguise and skilled hunters, they are also some of the cleverest builders in the animal kingdom. Ants build amazing underground nests where they live and keep their eggs.

22

Potter wasps make their nests from soil which they moisten with their own **saliva**. They shape the soil into a pot using their legs and their antennae.

When the pot is complete, the female wasp will hunt for beetle **larvae** and caterpillars which she paralyses with her sting and stores in the bottom of the pot. She will then lay a single egg there.

The egg hatches out into a larva, which feeds on the paralysed insects.

23

A female insect will lay hundreds of eggs during her life. The insect always lays her eggs close to a source of food for the larvae.

The eggs of the sexton beetle are laid in the carcass of a mouse, frog or other small, dead creature. The beetle efficiently buries the dead animal's body by digging the soil out from underneath it. This prevents other predators from eating the carcass before the eggs hatch.

Do insects ever look after their larvae?

A few species of insect take care of their larvae. The shield bug guards her eggs and stays with the larvae until they are grown.

Many incredible insects live in water. They all have ingenious ways of breathing underwater. Water beetles keep a supply of air underneath their wing cases. They use this to breathe and to keep afloat.

The water scorpion breathes through a snorkel at the end of its abdomen. It sticks this up through the surface of the water and into the open air.

This pond skater can walk on the surface of the water.

Why doesn't it sink?

The **surface tension** of the water creates a thin 'skin' which small water insects can stand on. The pond skater is also buoyed up by the tiny air bubbles clinging to the hairs all over its body.

Young land-living insects which closely resemble their parents when they are born are called nymphs. Young insects living in water are called naiads.

This is a dragonfly naiad; it's eating a small minnow.

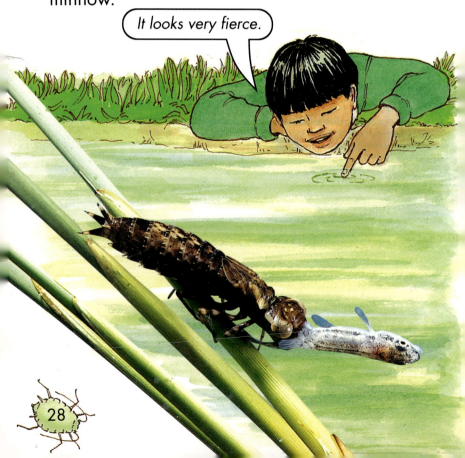

It looks very fierce.

When it is mature it will shed its skin and a beautiful dragonfly will emerge. The adult dragonfly will leave the water to live on land and in the air, taking its place alongside the other incredible insects of the world.

Can you name these insects? See if you can also remember what makes them so incredible. The answers are at the bottom of the page.

1.

2.

4.

3.

5.

6.

7.

1. Water beetle: keeps a supply of air underneath its wing case 2. Pond skater: can stand on the surface of water 3. Cicada: makes a noise by clicking the skin of its abdomen 4. Tiger beetle: fastest insect in the world 5. Dragonfly: has huge compound eyes that meet in the middle of its head 6. Sexton beetle: buries its prey 7. Hoverfly: its markings mimic a wasp.